A

PLAIN STATEMENT

OF THE

QUARREL WITH CANADA;

IN WHICH IS CONSIDERED

WHO

FIRST INFRINGED THE CONSTITUTION

OF

THE COLONY.

LONDON:
JAMES RIDGWAY AND SONS, PICCADILLY.
1838.

In the interest of creating a more extensive selection of rare historical book reprints, we have chosen to reproduce this title even though it may possibly have occasional imperfections such as missing and blurred pages, missing text, poor pictures, markings, dark backgrounds and other reproduction issues beyond our control. Because this work is culturally important, we have made it available as a part of our commitment to protecting, preserving and promoting the world's literature. Thank you for your understanding.

ON THE

QUARREL WITH CANADA.

In the course of a few days the Parliament of this country will be called upon, for the first time since many years, to pronounce upon a question involving many lives, affecting also the integrity of our empire and the character of our Government in the estimation of Foreign States. The question is, unhappily, to some extent, a party one, there being too many on one side who think to dispose of it by the word Treason; while others are not wanting who regard little else in the matter but the right of self-government, or what they value even more, the extension of Democracy. A few words written in no other spirit than that of justice, may be possibly not altogether without use to those who would consider before every thing, the real merits of the quarrel. But before we enter upon these, there are two points which we must assume; first, that there is such a thing as a right of dominion founded in conquest, which some seem reluctant to admit; as if a nation could ever grow powerful in any other way, and as if this, the only means of applying on a great scale the principle of association, had not tended upon the whole to the benefit of mankind. The other point we must take for granted is this: that a Colony is not, as soon as it has attained, perhaps only in its own opinion, the capacity of self-government, entitled, like a minor come of age, to turn round upon its parent or its guardian, and to say, We thank you for your past care, but for the future we are able and willing to take care of ourselves. We will assume, on the contrary, that though the tie is not to be perpetual, the parent state has a right, for some time at least, to profit by the maturity of that which it has fostered and protected, and that the colony is bound to repay, even in its prime, the debt which was contracted in its infancy. The payment, it is true, should be exacted in a fair and liberal spirit, and above all, the growth of the dependent state ought not to be checked, in order to retain it the longer in leading strings.

To apply this to Canada, which, succeeding as we did to the title of the French, we hold by the double right of colonization and of conquest: Can it be said we have abused, in her instance, our right as conquerors, when we have given her institutions as nearly after the model of our own as the difference between a ruling and a subject country would admit of? Or will it be pretended, either that we have not fulfilled towards her the duties we took upon ourselves of a guardian and protecting state, or that, setting aside her present alleged grievances, we have been upon the whole harsh or unreasonable in the payment we have exacted for our services? Money we have never asked, nor since our quarrel with America were we ever likely to do so; and if we have confined the trade of our colonists for our advantage, we have no less restricted our own for their benefit, and that in such a way as to hold out to them, at the same time, a premium for clearing their lands, and thereby in a two-fold manner adding to their wealth. In fact, for all that we have done to increase their riches in peace, and their strength in war, we have exacted little else in return but employment for our seamen, and to some extent also a field for our native industry and capital, from which the colony would derive as much benefit as ourselves.

But it is said, the debt, whatever it was, is cancelled by our ill usage. The plea if made out, is undoubtedly valid in its kind; for if it be true, that our domestic administration of the colony has been marked by habitual injustice or neglect towards the great bulk of its inhabitants, the people of this country ought not now to demand from unwilling Canada, that allegiance which they have fairly forfeited by the misconduct of their own servants. The account in that case should, if at all, be settled at home, between this country and its Ministers.

But how stands in truth the catalogue of Canadian grievances? By the confession of their own advocates they resolve themselves into two; the refusal of an Elective Council, and the recent alleged breach of the Colonial Constitution. Other grievances of a practical nature have it is true been brought forward, and have undoubtedly been proved to this extent, that there had been some jobbing ignorance and malversation in the government of the colony, and that the mischief, such as it was, arose in great measure from a corrupt and overbearing spirit in the legislative council.* These evils, however, if very great of their kind, cannot have been of very long duration, for it is admitted that, some twenty years ago, the rule of England was popular in Canada, and whatever abuses may have grown up in the interim, it cannot be denied that the Government has given proof of a disposition to correct them, and that there is enough, now in the House of Commons, of

* It is not only the House of Assembly, but in some cases also the Home Government, that have had to complain of the opposition of that body, they have represented on some occasions a party which might be called, without much injustice, the Orange party of Canada; but then, as that council is nominated by the governor, the remedy is in our hands, and the country is not therefore called upon to renounce a most imporant right.

Transatlantic patriotism, to prevent their recurrence, at least in any great degree. It is not therefore on these administrative wrongs that the Canadian House of Assembly are content to rest their quarrel, it is as was said before, upon the refusal of an Elective Council. That is to say, in other words, they were determined to provide in their own way for their future security; they had been ill-used by the Tories, and therefore they would not trust to the Whigs; they had been aggrieved by an unreformed Parliament, and therefore they looked for no redress from a reformed one; they had suffered wrong from England, indifferent or deceived, and therefore they hoped nothing from her justice, awakened and attentive; and because the constitution which we gave them, and which they had no right to make, has not excluded all abuse, they resolved upon obtaining a new one, by the very simple method of suspending the operation of that which they now have.

This brings us to the point, whether the right given to them by that constitution, of appropriating the net produce of certain duties to be levied in Canada under *acts of the British Parliament*, was ever meant, or can by possibility be supposed to have been meant, to answer such a purpose. Relying upon the apparent analogy of their constitution to ours, they contend that the right of appropriation carries with it the right of refusing to appropriate at all, that such right of refusal is altogether discretionary, and may according to the spirit of their constitution be converted to what use they think fit. But let us look first, to what use such a power is applicable among ourselves, and to what intent it was assumed: why chiefly, no doubt, to prevent or restrain the improper expenditure of the national monies, or more generally, as a check upon abuses of administration. And though we should admit, which is by no means clear, that it might *properly* be used by the House of Commons, as the means of extorting the assent of other branches of the Legislature, to the enactment of new laws, or even as it might be to a change in the constitution itself, yet if it were so used in this country, it would be against those who were competent to grant, what was sought to be enforced, and between those who had jointly the right of enacting what laws, and making what changes, might seem good in their eyes. Far different is the case in Canada; that constitution contains within itself no power of altering its fundamental laws, for it arose not from any supposed compact between the different parts of the Canadian people, it originated in the gift of the English Legislature, it rests upon a British act of Parliament,* and can only be altered, at least to the extent wished for, by those who gave it. It is not therefore against

* The 31st Geo. III. c. 31.

the Legislative Council, the other branch of their Parliament, it is not against the Governor as representing the Crown, that this stoppage of supplies is resorted to, in like manner as it might be here; for neither the Council nor the Governor have the right of assenting to the proposed change; but it is against us as a State, against an exterior and superior power, that this *constitutional* power of coercion, derived from our own gift, is now attempted to be turned.

It is, however, but fair to state, that the Canadian constitution has, since the passing of the act referred to, been altered by the Colonial Legislature, without any further consent than that of the Crown, and to this extent, that the numbers of the House of Assembly have been increased, and the benefit of representation extended to some districts of the Colony, which, on account of the thinness of their population, were not previously represented. Even this, perhaps, might have been questioned under the act above cited, in which the power it confers upon the Crown, of making laws, " with the consent and by the advice" of the Colonial Parliament, is qualified by the addition, " such laws not being repugnant to this act." There is, at any rate, a great difference between an alteration in the mode of using a right that had been conceded, which alteration was in effect nothing more than a carrying out of the act, in the spirit of the act itself, and doing that which is now sought to be obtained, which is, the taking away from this country an essential power expressly reserved to us, or to the Crown for our benefit, namely, the power of nominating the Legislative Council.* But even supposing that the King (or Queen) *in council*, would have the power of conceding this point, it could only be as the Sovereign of this country that he could have the right of giving up what belongs to us, or to the Crown for us, and no Ministry would ever dream of recommending such a step, without having first obtained the sanction of Parliament.

The matter then remains much as it was, in spite of the alleged precedent, and it is, after all, a claim of the Canadian House of Assembly, to exercise a *constitutional* control over the acts of the Imperial Legislature; and if we admit of such a pretence, it would be to say that the constitution which we freely bestowed upon the Canadians, and with such limits as were then thought necessary to

---

* The policy of retaining such a power, and the use we have made of it, are not now under consideration. The intention was, no doubt, to strengthen our rule, by securing one branch of the Colonial Legislature to that party in Canada which values, above every thing, the connexion with the mother country. Such a party is necessarily opposed in spirit to the natural tendencies of a prosperous colony; and the selections for the Council have, until very lately, been made too exclusively from among them: so much so, that the Council has in some instances proved itself more English than the chosen representative of the English Crown.

secure the connexion between us and them, might be endowed, as against us, and at the will of the donees, with a capability of indefinite expansion, and was in fact virtually a concession of complete independence. For if the Canadians are allowed the right of suspending their present Government, except on the terms which they may dictate, what is that but the right of making in all matters, and between them and us, such laws as they like? It would be idle for them to complain, that the analogy does not hold good in all points, between their constitution and ours; the answer to such a complaint is simply this, that *they* are the dependant state and *we* the sovereign.

But if it be asked, to what purpose then was this right of appropriating their public monies, conceded to them, the answer is also obvious; it was given to them as a means of control over the conduct of their executive, as a check upon corrupt expenditure, as a security against the malpractices of public servants; or if any alterations in the law *were* to be brought about by virtue of this right, through a stoppage of the supplies, it was such only as the domestic Legislature of the Colony, with the consent of its Governor, had the right of enacting. But, even for such purposes, a power so extraordinary was to be used sparingly and with discretion, and it was surely neither meant nor expected, that this, the " ultima ratio" of the English people, this dormant thunder of the British Parliament—which *we* talk of but use not—should ever become the common topic, the every-day weapon, of a Provincial Assembly.

It is clear, then, beyond a doubt, that that Assembly, by acting as they have done, have been the first to repudiate the constitution under which they exist, and have thereby restored us to those powers of a ruling state, which that constitution had alone abridged. And how have we used those powers? If we had, by our authority, levied taxes on the Canadians, for the purpose of administering the Government of that country, why, even then, we should but have enforced against them an obligation, to which, as colonists, they are undoubtedly liable. But we have done no such thing, we have not even released from a restraint improperly imposed monies already collected; we have but paid out of our own purse debts which ought long ago to have been discharged by them, but which in respect of our interest in the Colony, and of our share in its government were a claim also upon us. It was understood, no doubt at the time that the advance was to be made good, if necessary by act of Parliament, out of the monies now locked up in Canada; but before we thus directly infringed upon their right of appropriation, we gave them yet a year to consider.

So much for the question of Constitutional right, upon which the Canadians have thought fit, most unwisely, as I think, to rest their quarrel. By so doing, and by refusing to listen to any terms, or to enter upon any treaty, until this change in their constitution had been first conceded, they not only precluded *themselves* from any immediate relief, but they have given to their ill-wishers almost the right of saying, that they had no practical grievances at all. They had certainly not enough to justify them in rebellion, if that was their object at all events, but it is a bold assertion to say, that they had nothing to complain of whatever. One thing at any rate is clear from the recent insurrection, that the great bulk of the Canadian population is disaffected to our rule; it is all very well to talk of "the faction of Mr. Papineau," the faction of Mr. Papineau is the great majority of the Canadian people. And though no doubt the feeling by which they are animated has arisen in a great measure from the unjust desire of premature enfranchisement, it is far more than probable that they had some little wrong, at the hands of their Government. Some occasional neglect there must have been of colonial rights, (which rests not only in supposition) and to this we will readily believe were added, the habitual insolence of official exclusives, and the disregard of native worth and talent, of all such at any rate, as grew not within the pale of a most narrow circle. Nor is it a sufficient answer to this, that the sense of such wrongs is but lately awakened, and that it sprung from the very prosperity of which our Government was the source; for of what value are our benefits, if they bear not their natural fruits, and what gratitude is due to us for our improvements, if the capabilities we create, are shut out from their proper field? A people we may be sure do not rebel without some provocation, and if there be that rooted dislike to our dominion in the great bulk of the Canadians, that none but the most violent measures can bring them into subjection, and none but the most severe retain them in it, we should be very sure of the justice of our cause, before we resolve on such a course; one thing, at any rate, we should do well to consider, that we can hardly afford to own another Ireland.

It is hardly here the place, to discuss the arguments of those who would persuade us, that there is more to be gained, by commerce with a free state, than by the possession even of a peaceful Colony. The opinions of such men will have little weight in the decision of this question, for till other nations will consent also to overlook power in the pursuit of wealth, it is clearly not safe for us to act upon such a system, and no rational statesman will deny, that it is better for us to keep Canada in our hands, if she can be brought either through love or necessity to *acquiesce* in our rule. The attempt will at any rate be made, and so far as force alone is required for the purpose, it is obvious that the Government of this conntry *can* do in this matter, whatever the people will uphold them in doing.

A war, then, there must be, and one question only remains; upon what principle is that war to be carried on? If the question be rightly put, it contains its own answer. If there be a war, if there be a conflict between organised bodies, it should be carried on *as* a war. Too much by far has been said of treason in this case, and that by men who should think less of antiquated laws, and more of modern rights. Once, indeed, rebellion against the Sovereign, under any circumstances, and by whatever authority, was called treason, and it is still so written in our law books: but the only sort of resistance, which in a representative Government, justice and common sense will allow to be so called, and so punished, is the resistance of individuals to an united Legislature, or in other words, treason of this kind is now in name only a crime against the Sovereign, but is, in reality, a crime against the Constitution. It will not be said that, in this sense of the word, the Canadian insurgents are committing treason against the Constitution of Canada; for their Legislature is broken up, and in the dismemberment of that body, to which, when united, they owe their allegiance, each party is but clinging to the part, which he most loves. It makes little difference to the justice of the case, that the executive of the Colony, backed as it is by the resources of this country, has the power of crushing all opposition in its subjects; it is not the less true, that no legitimate object of obedience is to be found complete and unimpaired within the limits of Canada; and if the Canadian rebels are to be judged by their obligations to their own country, and to their own constitution, there would no more justice in hanging Mr. Papineau, than there would have been some two hundred years ago in the execution of Hampden or of Essex, had it been their fate to fall into the hands of the Royalists. Their case too was undoubtedly one of treason; but are there any Englishmen who think that their punishment would not have been murder? It may be said, however, that the House of Assembly have not lent such authority as they might lend, to the acts of their countrymen. That Assembly is now prorogued, but if we look back upon their proceedings for the last three years, if we bear in mind that they have repudiated by a series of votes, and by overwhelming majorities, the constitution as it stood, we shall hardly be bold enough to deny, that the standard of rebellion is, in fact, their standard; and unless we renounce the doctrine, that a people is represented by a majority of its citizens, we shall be compelled to admit, that the case of the Canadian insurgents, be it right or wrong, be it hopeless or triumphant, is the cause of the Canadian people. If, then, the acts of these men be not treason against Canada, it is hard to say that they are treason against us; for whatever subjection the collective body may be under to this country, the first duty of the individual colonist, is to his own legislature, the first claim upon his allegiance, is that of his own people.

That people, it is true, have been guilty of an offence against us; but the offence of one people against another is not treason, and, whatever it be called, it should be punished only as the offences of nations are punished, by war. Experience will soon teach the Canadians, that they were too few to be enemies, let not passion make us forget, that they are too many to be traitors. The ordinary incidents of the conflict, the usual consequences of a defeat, ending, as it probably will, if not in partial confiscation of their land, and in taxation of their products; yet, at least, in abridgment of their liberties, are enough surely for their punishment, and our security. Let us not, in the meantime, debase even the nature of civil war into the likeness of reciprocal murder. The usual arguments for the cutting off even of their leaders apply not to this case; for if we did visit upon their heads the offences of their followers, with what colour of truth could we pretend, that we did so for the sake of their countrymen whom they had deluded to their ruin? Would not the world see, it was the sacrifice of the chiefs of one people, to the interests of another; should not we feel, that it was vengeance we were inflicting, under the name and with the forms of justice? It is not thus, whatever we choose to make the issue of this contest, that it behoves us either to vindicate our quarrel, or to reassert our rights. If Canada is to return to her subjection, let us remember, that the blood of thousands slain in the field, is more easily forgiven, than that of one who dies upon the scaffold; and if, which *is possible*, we should find it expedient to yield up to our colonists, a dearly bought independence, let not the last memento we leave them of our rule, be the gibbet of those men, who whatever *we* may think of their character, will be ever regarded by their countrymen, as the authors of their nationality, the first assertors of their freedom.

The Canadians, on their side, would do well to consider in what spirit, and by what means the contest shall be maintained by them: the rifles of their Kentuckian friends may be useful, on an occasion; but their example is most dangerous. The punishment of a felonious warfare will be no less dreadful than deserved; and if the indignation of this country be once thoroughly awakened, it is not the power we should want, to drive out from the richest portions of Canada, a race of *worse* than rebels: the number wanted to supply their place would be little missed here, and with the land ready cultivated to their hands, they would need but little help from home to profit by the gift, and to make good their title.

SUPPLEMENT.

The foregoing pages were meant chiefly as an argument upon the question of the constitutional right to stop the supplies. It should however be borne in mind, that a fair judgment upon the *whole* merits of the question cannot be formed, without an inquiry also into the grievances alleged as the provocation to such a step.

The chief of these as stated by the advocates consist:—

1. In the appointment as Judges of men objectionable on the score of incapacity or party spirit, of which Judges Gale, Thompson, and Fletcher, are cited as instances. The appointment of the first is stated to have been disallowed by Mr. Spring Rice as Colonial Secretary, but he was continued by Lord Aylmer, and still remains upon the Bench.

2. The irresponsibility of the Judges to the House of Assembly, and there being allowed to sit in the Legislative and Executive Councils, from which, it must be added, that owing to the feeling shewn, most of them have *voluntarily* retired.

3. The non-existence of a good Jury Law, the improved Jury Law having expired, and its renewal having failed, owing to the opposition of the Legislative Council to the measures of the House of Assembly.

4. The impunity of offenders and peculators connected with, or protected by, the official party, of which the strongest instances are—A gaoler, who was indicted by the Attorney-General for the murder of a prisoner under his charge, who was said to have died of cold. The bill was thrown out by a Grand Jury, said to have been packed

by the Sheriff (Gugy), whose officer the accused party was; a Land-Commissioner, accused of fraud to a large extent, in the discharge of his office, but who escaped with the loss of his situation; and, lastly, the case of a great public defaulter, (Sir John Caldwell) whose property was protected from the full and proper consequences of his default.

5. The exclusive distribution of patronage, and the plurality of offices held by the same persons.

6. The existence and conduct of the British and American Land Company, of which the Act is said to have been passed without fair notice or publicity, and in the shape of a private Act, and by means of which those funds were drawn into the hands of an English Association, which ought, it is pretended, to have been subject to the control of the House of Assembly, and which has been the means of bringing into the Colony destitute and unhealthy emigrants, for resisting whose introduction the House of Assembly has been represented as hostile to the immigration of Englishmen.

7. The refusal to place at the disposal of the House of Assembly the *whole* of the revenues of the Colony, which, together with the refusal of an Elective Council, and the defects of the Judicial system, makes up the three capital grievances of the Canadians.

The immediate provocation to revolt is said to be found in the dismissal of magistrates and militia officers, for attending meetings, held for the purpose of remonstrating against the resolutions of the House of Commons.

THE END.

NORMAN AND SKEEN, PRINTERS, MAIDEN LANE, COVENT GARDEN.

Printed by Libri Plureos GmbH in Hamburg, Germany